THE AMERICAN WEST
IN THE THIRTIES

122 Photographs by
Arthur Rothstein

Dover Publications, Inc.
New York

FRONTISPIECE: Bleached skull of a steer on the dry, sunbaked earth of the Bad Lands, South Dakota, 1936.

Published in Canada by General Publishing Company, Ltd., 30 Lesmill Road, Don Mills, Toronto, Ontario.
Published in the United Kingdom by Constable and Company, Ltd., 10 Orange Street, London WC2H 7EG.

The American West in the Thirties: 122 Photographs by Arthur Rothstein is a new work, first published by Dover Publications, Inc., in 1981.

DOVER *Pictorial Archive* SERIES

International Standard Book Number: 0-486-24106-8
Library of Congress Catalog Card Number: 80-69566

Manufactured in the United States of America
Dover Publications, Inc.
180 Varick Street
New York, N.Y. 10014

THE PHOTOGRAPHS

As a photojournalist for more than 45 years, I have had the opportunity to photograph the people and places of this varied and vibrant world.

The photographs in this volume are from my years as photographer for the Farm Security Administration. My job was to photograph small towns, rural areas and general agricultural conditions throughout the country. From 1935 to 1940, my travels took me through every state in the U.S.A.

In photographing for the Farm Security Administration, I became conscious of a new concept—that photographs could be used to communicate ideas and emotions, as well as present facts, for the camera captures the decisive moment and records events with greater accuracy than does the human eye.

My photography is based on the concept of knowing the subject and telling the story as graphically as I can. I use design and composition to enhance the effect and make the message clear. I prefer to portray people with dignity and sympathy and to capture expressions with the greatest meaning. Sometimes I will select a revealing detail or fragment of the whole scene in order to make a more effective statement. My photographs are primarily designed to serve a useful purpose in communication, yet many of them have been considered works of art.

Because powerful images are fixed in the mind more readily than words, the photographer needs no interpreter. A photograph means the same thing all over the world and no translator is required. Photography is truly a universal language, transcending all boundaries of race, politics and nationality.

The photographer who uses this universal language has a great social responsibility. Accepting this challenge, I have probed the problems of our times and used my camera to communicate ideas, facts and emotions.

For those who see my photographs in this volume, I hope that these images will be a remembrance of the past, a record of accomplishment and an affirmation of faith in humanity.

ARTHUR ROTHSTEIN

New York, 1981

THE PHOTOGRAPHER

Born in New York City in 1915, Arthur Rothstein is a graduate of Columbia University, where he was a founder of the University Camera Club and photographic editor of *The Columbian*. Rothstein joined the Farm Security Administration in 1935 and for the next five years made some of the most significant documentary photographs ever taken of rural and small-town America. He became a staff photographer at *Look* magazine in 1940, but left shortly after to join the Office of War Information and then the Army, which took him for three years to the China-Burma-India theater. In 1946 he rejoined *Look* as Director of Photography.

Currently, he is Director of Photography of *Parade*, the Sunday newspaper magazine, with responsibility for photography, picture research, feature-story production and editorial illustration.

Rothstein is a member of the New York Press Photographers Association, the National Press Photographers Association and Photographic Administrators (of which he is past President). He is a founder and former officer of the American Society of Magazine Photographers. In 1968 he was named a Fellow of the Royal Photographic Society of Great Britain, the oldest photographic society in the world.

He has been a member of the faculty of the Graduate School of Journalism at Columbia University and has also lectured at other universities, workshops and conferences.

The author of numerous magazine articles, Rothstein has written three technical books, *Photojournalism* (1956, revised 1965, 1969, 1974, 1979), an authoritative account of the methods used to produce photographs for magazines and newspapers; *Creative Color* (1963), an analysis of ideas and devices used in modern color photography; and *Color Photography Now* (1970), a survey of current practices and techniques in color photography. In 1967 he collaborated with William Saroyan on a book about the U.S.A. called *Look At Us*. An earlier collection of his Farm Security Administration photographs was published by Dover in 1978 as *The Depression Years as Photographed by Arthur Rothstein*. The volume *Words and Pictures by Arthur Rothstein* appeared in 1979.

The photographs of Arthur Rothstein are in the permanent collection of major museums. Exhibitions of his work have been presented at the Smithsonian Institution, Washington; the Museum of Modern Art, New York; the International Museum of Photography, Rochester; the Royal Photographic Society, London; and the Bibliothèque Nationale, Paris.

Cowhand, William Tonn Ranch, Custer County, Montana, 1939.

2   Roundup, William Tonn Ranch, Custer County, Montana, 1939.

Cattle at a water hole, Dawes County, Nebraska, 1939.

Cattle grazing, Ouray County, Colorado, 1939.

Cows and calves leaving a corral after branding, Three Circle Ranch
roundup, Powder River County, Montana, 1939.

6   Feeding cattle at a stockyard, Scottsbluff, Nebraska, 1939.

Driving cattle in a corral, William Tonn Ranch, Custer County, Montana, 1939.

Branding calves in a corral, William Tonn Ranch, Custer County, Montana, 1939.

Branding a calf, William Tonn Ranch, Custer County, Montana, 1939.

10   Rancher, Powder River County, Montana, 1939.

Hay stacker, Teton County, Wyoming, 1936.

Ranch hand resting on a haystack, Dangberg Ranch, Douglas County,
Nevada, 1940.

Loading hay, Dangberg Ranch, Douglas County, Nevada, 1940.

OPPOSITE: Entrance to the mess hall, Quarter Circle U Ranch, near Birney, Montana, 1939. ABOVE: Cook at the roundup, Three Circle Ranch, Powder River County, Montana, 1939.

16   Ranch hands at dinner, Quarter Circle U Ranch, near Birney, Montana, 1939.

Cowhands singing after a day's work at the roundup, Quarter Circle U
Ranch, near Birney, Montana, 1939.

Walter Latta, Bozeman, Montana, 1939.

Cowhand trying a saddle at the Capriola Saddlery, Elko, Nevada, 1940. 19

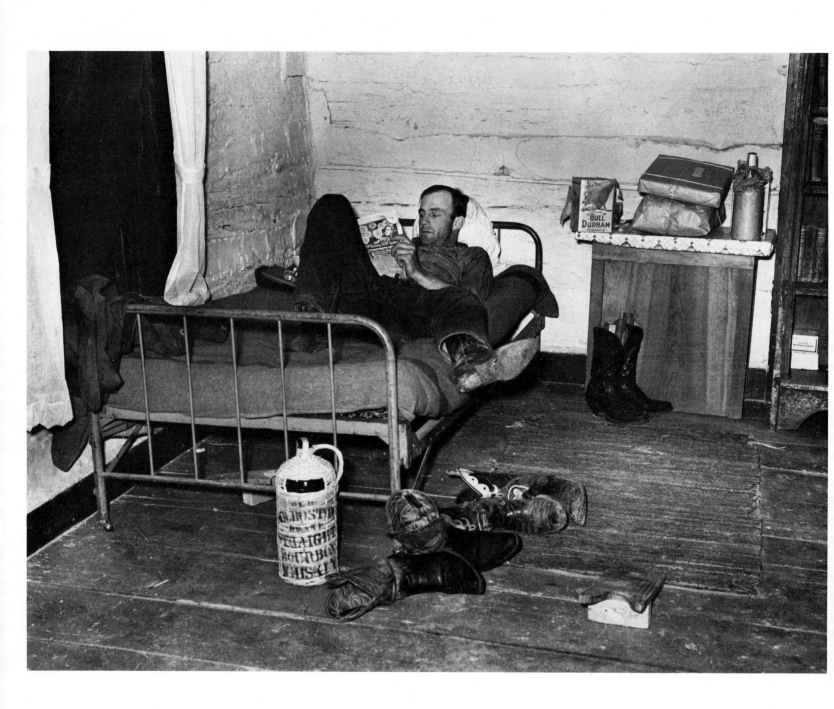

Ranch hand in the bunkhouse, Brewster, Montana, 1939.

Mare and colt, Warren Brewster Ranch, Montana, 1939.

OPPOSITE: Shearing sheep, Idaho, 1936. ABOVE: In the lambing shed,
Dangberg Ranch, Douglas County, Nevada, 1940.

24   Sheepherder's wagon, Montana, 1939.

Basque sheepherder camped on the range, Dangberg Ranch, Douglas
County, Nevada, 1940.

Sheepherder watching his flock, Madison County, Montana, 1939.

Winter wheat harvest, Whitman County, Washington, 1936.

Farmer, Lancaster County, Nebraska, 1936.

Gangplow, Pine Ridge, Nebraska, 1936.

30 ABOVE: Hay meadow, Eagle County, Colorado, 1939. OPPOSITE: Melting snow, Hayes County, Nebraska, 1940.

Farm, Hayes County, Nebraska, 1940.

New farm home, Douglas County, Nebraska, 1936.

OPPOSITE: Tom Reilly, farmer, near Hotchkiss, Colorado, 1939.
ABOVE: Resettled farmer, Douglas County, Nebraska, 1936.

Farmer's wife in her new storage cellar, Falls City, Nebraska, 1936.

Log barn, Cherokee County, Kansas, 1936.

ABOVE: Field worker with a knife used in topping sugar beets, Adams County, Colorado, 1939. OPPOSITE: President of the farmers' cooperative, Fairbury Farmsteads, Nebraska, 1936.

Farmer resettled at Douglas County Farmsteads, Nebraska, 1936.

Farmer's son with a prize 4H Club calf, Fairbury Farmsteads, Nebraska, 1936.   41

42   Son of an evicted sharecropper, Butler County, Missouri, 1939.

Children of an evicted sharecropper, Butler County, Missouri, 1939.

Wife of a resettled farmer, Falls City, Nebraska, 1936.

Wife of a resettled farmer, Kearney, Nebraska, 1936. 45

Moving into a new house, Douglas County, Nebraska, 1936.

Pioneer settler in her sod house, Cimarron County, Oklahoma, 1936.

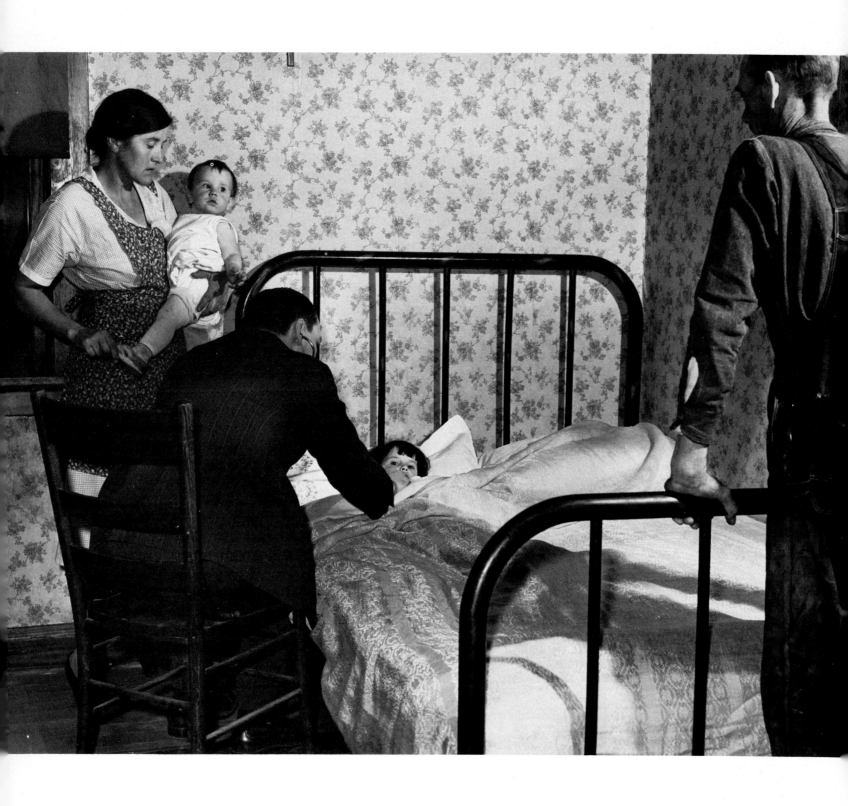

ABOVE: Physician visiting a farm home, St. Charles County, Missouri, 1939.
OPPOSITE: School is over, Bucoda, Missouri, 1939.

Nursery school, Tulare, California, 1938.

President of the farmer's cooperative, Loup City Farmsteads, Nebraska, 1936.

Fireman, Carson City, Nevada, 1940.

Frank Latta, old-time cowpuncher, Bozeman, Montana, 1939.

Empty farm and idle truck (typical of the drought area), Beach, North
Dakota, 1936.

Submarginal farm, Oneida County, Idaho, 1936.   55

Son of a dust-bowl farmer, Liberal, Kansas, 1936.

Drifts of soil piled up by dust-bowl winds against a farmer's barn, Liberal,
Kansas, 1936.

Farmer who abandoned his home and moved into a dugout near town to become eligible for relief, Grassy Butte, North Dakota, 1936.

Cooperative gas station, Shafter Migrant Camp, Shafter, California, 1940.

Homestead on submarginal land, Pennington County, South Dakota, 1936.

Corn withered by drought and chewed by grasshoppers, Terry, Montana, 1939.

62   Dead longhorn, aftermath of drought, Sioux County, Nebraska, 1936.

Skeleton of horse, Dawes County, Nebraska, 1936.

Skunk cabbage and stumps are obstacles to clearing an abandoned homestead, Oregon, 1936.

Cutting trees for fence posts, Pine Ridge, Nebraska, 1936.

ABOVE: Logs on the Columbia River, Longview, Washington, 1936.
OPPOSITE: Copper pit, Ruth, Nevada, 1940.

Rocky Mountain George, 68-year-old prospector, Esmeralda County, Nevada, 1940.

Pouring gold, El Dorado Canyon, Clark County, Nevada, 1940.

Old mine office, Virginia City, Nevada, 1940.

Cemetery, Tonopah, Nevada, 1940.

Hotel De Paris, Georgetown, Colorado, 1939.

Hotel De Paris, Georgetown, Colorado, 1939.

74   Spanish mission church, Taos, New Mexico, 1936.

Taos Pueblo, New Mexico, 1936.

Taos Pueblo, New Mexico, 1936.

Governor Sandoval, Taos Pueblo, New Mexico, 1936.

Calamity Jane's Rock, Custer State Park, South Dakota, 1936.

Badlands National Park, South Dakota, 1936.

Teton National Forest, Wyoming, 1936.

Rock formation, Valley of Fire, Clark County, Nevada, 1940.

OPPOSITE: Badlands in the Panamint Range, Death Valley, California, 1940.
ABOVE: Rock formation, Laramie County, Wyoming, 1940.

Sunset, Imperial, Nebraska, 1940.

Snow fence, Summit County, Utah, 1940.

Butte, Montana, 1939.

Butte, Montana, 1939.

Above: Meaderville, Montana, 1939. Opposite: Wall, South Dakota, 1936.

Saloon, Beowawe, Nevada, 1940.

Miner's Union Hall, Silver City, Nevada, 1940.

Stores on the main street of Elko, Nevada, 1940.

Silver Peak, Nevada, 1940.

Going to church, Grassy Butte, North Dakota, 1936.

Closed general store, Grassy Butte, North Dakota, 1936.

Main Street, Austin, Nevada, 1940.

Main Street, Fairfield, Montana, 1939.

Virginia City, Montana, 1939.

Blacksmith shop, Virginia City, Montana, 1939.

Main Street, Eureka, Nevada, 1940.

Medicine Bow, Wyoming, 1940.

Waiting with the mail for the train to Reno, Minden, Nevada, 1940.

Fire Department, Austin, Nevada, 1940.

ABOVE: Gas station on the Colorado-Wyoming state line, 1940.
OPPOSITE: Miners lounging in front of the Arcade, Butte, Montana, 1939.

ABOVE: General store, Pony, Montana, 1939. OPPOSITE: County Court House, Kansas, 1936.

High-school boys in their jalopy, Genoa, Nevada, 1940.

Former blacksmith shop used for auto repairs, Glendive, Montana, 1939.   109

PROJECT PARLOR INC.
DRINKS
CANDY   TOBACCO   ICE CREAM

DRINK
Coca-Cola

Copenhagen
's nuff said

UNION
LEADER
for
PIPE OR CIGAR

Opposite: Fairfield, Montana, 1939. Above: Bar in the Carson Brewery, Carson City, Nevada, 1940.

111

ABOVE: Drover's Hotel opposite the stockyards, Kansas City, Kansas, 1936.
OPPOSITE: Main Street, Las Vegas, Nevada, 1940.

BAR
Apache
Casino
Beautiful COCKTAIL LOUNGE
delightful entertainment....
765
Apache

ABOVE: Bingo players, Las Vegas, Nevada, 1940. OPPOSITE: Roulette players, Las Vegas, Nevada, 1940.

OPPOSITE: Gold-mine office, El Dorado Canyon, Clark County, Nevada,
1940. ABOVE: Ghost town, Rhyolite, Nevada, 1940.

Auction, Kearney, Nebraska, 1936.

Rally for the Townsend Plan of old-age pensions, Kansas, 1936.

Auction, Kearney, Nebraska, 1936.

Fairfield, Montana, 1939.